SEQUOYAH
Cherokee Hero

by Joanne Oppenheim
illustrated by Bert Dodson

Troll Associates

Troll Associates

Library of Congress Catalog Card Number: 78-60117
ISBN 0-89375-159-6

10   9   8   7   6   5   4   3   2

SEQUOYAH
Cherokee Hero

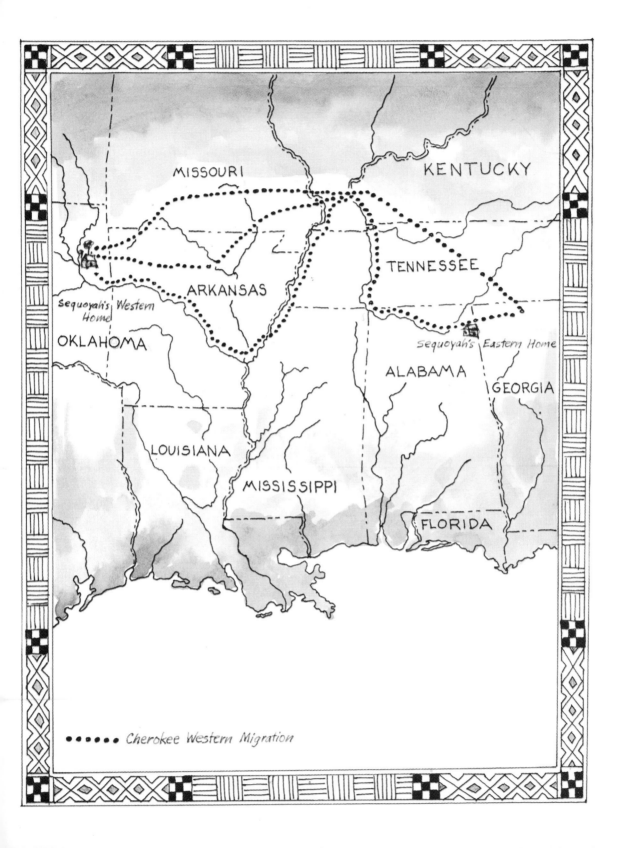

MISSOURI

KENTUCKY

TENNESSEE

ARKANSAS

Sequoyah's Western Home

OKLAHOMA

Sequoyah's Eastern Home

ALABAMA

GEORGIA

LOUISIANA

MISSISSIPPI

FLORIDA

•••••• Cherokee Western Migration

Sequoyah erased the pictures he had been drawing in the earth. He knew he should finish tending the rows of corn in the garden. There were many chores he still had to do before he could play with the other children.

The warm August sun seemed to call him away from his work. He thought of the racing and wrestling games the others would be playing, and he sighed.

Sequoyah had little time for play. There was work to be done.

Sometimes he felt sad. He thought of his father, a trader who had gone back to live with his own people.

Sequoyah and his mother, Wur-teh, lived near the Cherokee village of Taskigi, in the Smoky Mountains of Tennessee. Strangers often visited their small cabin to trade scissors, knives, needles, and cloth for the Indians' furs.

They brought stories of faraway places that made Sequoyah wonder about the great world outside his little village.

6

Secretly, Sequoyah dreamed that one day his father would return. But Wur-teh had given up such dreams. There was corn to be planted, wood to be cut, and food to be cooked. Cherokees called this "woman's work," but Wur-teh needed her son's help.

When his chores were done, Sequoyah sometimes spent time with the medicine men. He
learned where to find the special herbs and roots
they used to heal the sick. He had a good memory,
and soon knew the name of every plant and how
it was used.

Listening to the stories of the medicine men, he drew pictures in his mind. Like most children, he daydreamed about what he would be when he grew up.

Maybe he would work spells and make good medicine. Or maybe he would be a brave warrior! Perhaps he would even learn to use the "talking leaves"—the books he had seen at the schools of the settlers. He often wondered what special magic allowed people to talk to each other by making marks on paper.

9

As the seasons passed, Sequoyah worked more and more with his hands. Wur-teh sent him often to trade in other villages. There he saw silver-smiths working with hammers and tools. He was quick to learn how to melt silver and shape the hot liquid into spoons, bracelets, and buttons.

Before long, he hurried home with tools of his own. He could hardly wait to try to shape and decorate the gleaming silver.

Wur-teh smiled as Sequoyah worked. He etched tiny deer and flying birds on the handles of knives and spoons, and made jewelry for his people to wear.

Sequoyah was proud when traders asked who had made such beautiful things. But still, he thought, such work would not make him a leader.

For several years, Sequoyah made journeys back and forth to other villages. Often, on the trail, he saw settlers' wagons rolling west. Every year, more boats traveled on the river.

Sequoyah did not speak the words of the white people. He just watched more and more of their boats and wagons coming.

But in the villages, he saw many of his people taking up the white men's ways. He was sad that Cherokees would turn from the old ways.

Then, a greater sadness filled his heart. Wur-teh grew old and died. He was lonely in their house. The chair he had made for her was empty now.

Sequoyah could not stay there any longer. For two years, he moved from one village to another.

Finally, he settled in Alabama in the village of Coosa.

Before long, Sequoyah married a Cherokee woman named Utiya. Their house was neat, and their garden was full of vegetables and flowers.

In his travels, he had learned the skills of a blacksmith. Now, in Coosa, he built his own forge. His days were busy as he shoed horses and mended guns. When people needed a silversmith or blacksmith, they came to Sequoyah.

15

But an idea was growing in his mind. Whenever he had a spare moment, he thought about how he could make picture-words that all the Cherokees could read and understand. If the white people could talk with their marks, why couldn't the Cherokees?

As the years passed, Sequoyah became well known in Coosa and nearby villages. Often, he sat with the Cherokee leaders at their council lodge.

Smoking his long clay pipe, Sequoyah listened as they spoke of the white men's treaties. Indians could not read the white men's "talking leaves." They called them magic.

"It is no magic," Sequoyah said. "Look, I will make marks for Cherokee words. Then, we will have the same magic!"

Many of the council leaders laughed at Sequoyah, but he did not care. One day, he promised himself, he would be able to write down every word in the Cherokee language.

16

But Sequoyah had little time to work on his Cherokee writing. In 1812, the Americans and English were at war. Sequoyah rode off to fight for the Americans. His skills as a blacksmith were needed in the faraway camps of Georgia.

At night, he watched the soldiers writing letters to their wives and children. Sometimes, he would see them smile as they read letters from home.

Cherokee warriors could not send talking leaves. Some day, he thought, I will give my people this magic.

19

When the war was over, Sequoyah returned to Coosa. Utiya was happy to have him home, but her happiness did not last for long.

Sequoyah was acting strangely. Day after day, month after month, he did nothing but work on his alphabet.

"Look," he said to his children. "I am making a picture for every word in the Cherokee language."

"But the roof is leaking! The garden is full of weeds!" Utiya scolded.

Still Sequoyah worked. Soon every corner of the cabin was filled with piles of pictures.

Sequoyah could see that there were too many pictures and too many words. He would have to find an easier way.

One day he took his daughter Ah-yo-ka for a walk in the woods. They listened to the birds singing, and he began to repeat their sounds. Each bird had its own song, but some sounds were the same.

Suddenly, he knew that sounds were the magic key to the Cherokee language!

"Listen, Ah-yo-ka!"

Slowly, he said his name. He broke it apart into syllables—Se-quo-yah. With a twig from a tree, he made marks in the sand. He made a different mark for each syllable.

Then he said other words. Some words had the same sounds. He could use the same marks for these sounds.

"Come, little one. I have found the magic!"

He worked quickly. New piles of bark were
scattered all over the cabin. He worked night and
day.

Utiya could stand it no longer. "You are a fool,
Sequoyah. You do nothing but play with pieces of
bark. I do not know you any more!"

Then, in anger, she threw the stacks of bark
into the blazing fireplace.

24

Sequoyah took Ah-yo-ka and found an empty cabin in the woods. He was not ready to give up his dream.

One day, Ah-yo-ka found a book lying in the grass, not far from their cabin. Sequoyah could not read it, but he studied it day after day. He saw that there were twenty-six marks used over and over again. But twenty-six letters were not enough for all the Cherokees' word-sounds. Soon, he made up new symbols.

Again, the stacks of tree bark were growing!

Back in Coosa, there was much gossip about Sequoyah's strange ideas. The people remembered how he had spent many of his boyhood days with the medicine men.

Now, they rode past his cabin and heard the Cherokee word-sounds he repeated again and again.

"He is working bad spells!" they said.

One day, while Sequoyah was in the woods with Ah-yo-ka, several people from the village rode to his cabin.

Looking at the piles of bark with the strange marks on them, they shook their heads.

"He is making bad magic," they said. "We must get rid of him!"

They set fire to the cabin.

In the fiery blaze, they destroyed all his long years of work.

Ah-yo-ka wept when she saw the ruined cabin. Sequoyah held her close as she sobbed.

"Do not cry, little one. All is not lost."

Sequoyah's memory was good—he remembered every sign he had made for the Cherokee language.

Carefully, he marked them, one by one, on a large piece of buckskin.

30

Now Sequoyah knew that he must leave Alabama. Many Cherokees were moving west to the Oklahoma and Arkansas territory. He and Ah-yo-ka would join them. Maybe they would find a home there and be able to finish the Cherokee alphabet.

Their move west was a happy change for both Sequoyah and his young daughter. On their way, they met a young Cherokee woman named Sally. She was kind to Ah-yo-ka, and she did not laugh at Sequoyah's dream.

In time, Sequoyah built a small cabin in the wilderness. There he continued to work long hours on his alphabet. He knew he had to simplify it. "There are two hundred symbols," he sighed. "That is too many."

Still, he kept on working, and Ah-yo-ka worked with him. She learned how to read every mark he wrote.

At last, the alphabet was finished. With eighty-six symbols, Sequoyah could write every word in the Cherokee language!

"I must take my work back to the East," he told Sally. "It is a gift I will bring to the Tribal Council."

Sally was afraid to see him go. She feared the people who had burned his cabin. Maybe they would do even worse things now!

But Sequoyah would not change his mind.

"I will be safe," he told her. "When I have taught my people the magic of their own language, I will return. I will take Ah-yo-ka with me, and she will help me convince them that reading and writing will make us one people again."

With Ah-yo-ka, Sequoyah began the long trip over the lands and waters that led to their old homeland. They brought greetings from the members of the Western Nation of Cherokees to their friends and relatives in the East.

When Ah-yo-ka and Sequoyah reached Tennessee, they did not like the looks on the faces of the men in the Tribal Council. The leaders muttered and shook their heads as Sequoyah showed them his alphabet.

Sequoyah wrote down some words and handed them to Ah-yo-ka. She read them.

"It is a trick!" they shouted. "He has put a spell on the child!"

"It is no trick," said Sequoyah. "It is no spell. I will prove it. Take Ah-yo-ka to the far end of the village. While she is gone, I will write down anything you say. When she returns, she will be able to read it."

No one believed Sequoyah. They were sure his magic would fail. So Ah-yo-ka was led out of the council house.

36

Silence filled the room when Ah-yo-ka returned. Sequoyah said nothing as he handed the paper to his young daughter.

Ah-yo-ka's hands trembled. It was up to her now. She must not fail her father and his long years of work.

Her heart pounded as she read every word he had written.

"It is true!" they shouted. "The talking leaves speak in Cherokee!"

There were tears of joy in Sequoyah's eyes as he smiled at Ah-yo-ka. She had helped him make his dream come true.

For many months, Sequoyah and Ah-yo-ka were busier than ever. Everyone wanted to learn how to read and write. Week after week, Indians came from nearby villages. They learned quickly. When they returned to their homes, they taught others.

Before long, Sequoyah's symbols were painted on rocks, fences, and the sides of houses. Everyone—old people, young people, women and men—learned how to use the new alphabet.

Finally, their work in the East was done. It was time to leave. When Sequoyah and Ah-yo-ka returned home, they brought letters that had been written by the Eastern Cherokees to their friends and families in the Western Nation.

Before long, almost all of the Cherokees had learned to read and write.

In time, they started their own newspaper, called the *Cherokee Phoenix*. Now they could read news from all parts of the world. The scattered Cherokee people were united by the words of the printed page.

The Cherokee Nation now looked upon Sequoyah as a great leader. At the Tribal Council, they gave him a beautiful silver medal carved with two crossed pipes. The pipes were the symbols of the Eastern and Western Cherokees he had brought together through his alphabet.

Sequoyah's dreams of helping the Cherokees had come true. He had been able to lead his people, not as a warrior or medicine man, but as the giver of the precious gift of reading and writing.

Sequoyah lived to see great changes come to his land and his people. His alphabet became the key to a new feeling of brotherhood and understanding among all the Cherokees. And, thanks to his talking leaves, the old stories and ways of the Cherokees did not die.

His dream had become real. He had done something no one else had ever done. He was the first person in history to invent a written language alone.

For this great gift to the Cherokee Nation, the name of Sequoyah will never be forgotten.

In spite of the spirit of understanding the Cherokees received through the gift of Sequoyah, they suffered terrible hardships in the troubled years that followed. In about 1830, gold was discovered in the eastern territory. Wagons rolled endlessly across Cherokee cornfields and hunting grounds. The government used every means possible to force the Indians off their lands. With heavy hearts, the tribes moved westward. They moved on foot, in wagons, and on horseback to a land they did not know. Unified now in their sorrow, almost one-third of the Cherokee people died on this long and painful "trail of tears."